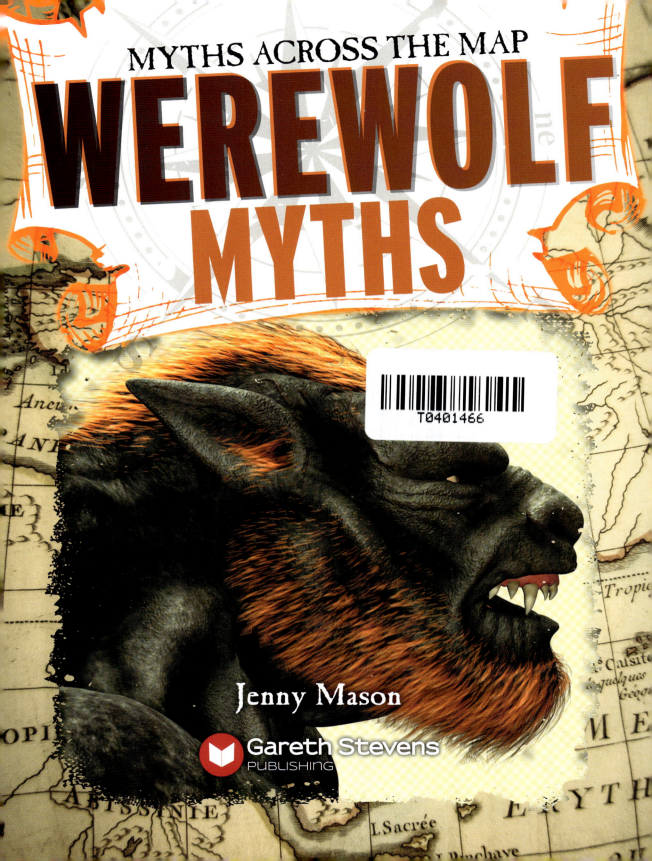

MYTHS ACROSS THE MAP
WEREWOLF MYTHS

Jenny Mason

Gareth Stevens
PUBLISHING

Please visit our website, **www.garethstevens.com**.
For a free color catalog of all our high-quality books,
call toll free 1-800-542-2595 or fax 1-877-542-2596.

CATALOGING-IN-PUBLICATION DATA

Names: Mason, Jenny.
Title: Werewolf myths / Jenny Mason.
Description: New York : Gareth Stevens Publishing, 2018. | Series: Myths across the map | Includes index.
Identifiers: LCCN ISBN 9781538214497 (pbk.) | ISBN 9781538213766 (library bound) | ISBN 9781538214794 (6 pack)
Subjects: LCSH: Werewolves--Juvenile literature. | Animals, Mythical--Juvenile literature.
Classification: LCC GR830.W4 M37 2018 | DDC 398.24'54--dc23

Published in 2018 by
Gareth Stevens Publishing
111 East 14th Street, Suite 349
New York, NY 10003

Copyright © 2018 Gareth Stevens

Project Manager: Adrianna Edwards
Editor: Ron Edwards
Design and Composition: Ruth Dwight
Copy editors: Adrianna Edwards, Francine Geraci
Media Researchers: Adrianna Edwards, Paula Joiner, Maddi Nixon
Proofreader: Francine Geraci
Index: Ron Edwards, Maddi Nixon

PHOTO CREDITS: Credit Abbreviations: S Shutterstock; WC Wikimedia Commons. Position on the page: L: left, R: right. Cover, Title Page: Bob Orsillo/S; 4: breakermaximus/S; 5: Andrea Danti/S; 6: tan_tan/S; 7: Lupa/S; 8: Fogey/S; 9: Mircea C/S; 10: schankz/S; 11: Ramon Carretero/S; 12: Tommyknocker at English Wikipedia/WC; 13: Zvereva Iana/S; 14: Vuk Kostic/S; 15: Kiselev Andrey Valerevich/S; 16: Brian Patterson Photos/S; 17: breakermaximus/S; 18: Vuk Kostic/S; 19: Tinseltown/S; 20 L: Audrey Snider-Bell/S, R: dptro/S; 21: Marcin Sylwia Ciesielski/S; 22 L: guentermanaus/S, R: Martin Fowler/S; 23: Neirfy/S; 24: Christian Lagerek/S; 25 L: Sarawoot/S, R: Sergio Bertino/S; 26: Satirus/S; 27: Heike Rau/S; 28: Carlo2017/S; 29: Baronb/S; 30: Kateryna Kon/S; 31: Victoria Antonova/S; 32: Barandash Karandashich/S; 33: dezignor/S; 34: vasara/S; 35: Hyde, James Nevins and Montgomery, Frank Hugh. A practical treatise on diseases of the skin, for the use of students and practitioners. Philadelphia, New York: Lea brothers & co. 1897. 478. Internet Archive. Web. 16 May 2017; 36: Manfred Ruckszio/S; 37: Everett Historical/S; 38: Plan, Pierre Paul. Jacques Callot, maître graveur (1593-1635) suivi d'un catalogue chronologique. Bruxelles: G. van Oest. 1914. 89 verso. Internet Archive. Web 16 May 2017; 39, 40, 41: Everett Historical/S; 42: RikoBest/S; 43: Everett Collection/S; 44: N.G.Artsy/S; 45: vectorEps/S; Design Elements: Margarita Miller/S, viewgene/S, yoshi0511/S.

All rights reserved. No part of this book may be reproduced in any form without permission from the publisher, except by a reviewer.

Printed in the United States of America
CPSIA compliance information: Batch CW18GS: For further information contact Gareth Stevens, New York, New York at 1-800-542-2595.

TABLE OF CONTENTS

WHAT IS A WEREWOLF? 4

GOING TO THE DOGS 6

BELIEFS UNLEASHED 13

MARKING TERRITORY 21

DIGGING UP THE TRUTH 29

LEADER OF THE PACK 37

WEREWOLF MYTHS ACROSS THE MAP 45

GLOSSARY 46

FURTHER INFORMATION 47

INDEX 48

WHAT IS A WEREWOLF?

AN ICON

Werewolf. You would know it if you saw it (and lived to tell about it). A werewolf is a person who morphs into a bloodthirsty, wolflike monster in the light of a full moon. People around the world recognize this iconic nightmare because it is such an enduring myth.

Myths are commonly held beliefs rooted deep in the past. They are the stories we tell ourselves to explain the inexplicable. Myths can also teach important lessons.

The myth of the werewolf arose at least 1,000 years before Christianity.

FAST FACT
Myths remind us that humans are capable of both good and evil.

IN CASE YOU *WER* WONDERING

People who study the origins of words have struggled to pin down the exact meaning of the werewolf's name. *Wer*, or *were*, links back to the Old English word for "man." But it also appears in other related languages. The Goths said *wair*. The Franks used *uuara*. The Celts uttered *gur*, *gwr*, or *ur*. *Verr* was used in Old Norse, and *vira* in Persian and in ancient Sanskrit.

In all these variations, the word implied more than "man." It signified warriors. It also suggested armies, destruction, cruelty, and hostility. Perhaps the old languages could not speak of humankind without acknowledging its dark side.

BEWARE OF WOLVES!

Some scholars have suggested *wer* links to the root word "-ware," as in "beware." "Little Red Riding Hood," "The Three Little Pigs," and "The Wolf and the Seven Goats" are all fairy tales warning children to beware of wolves.

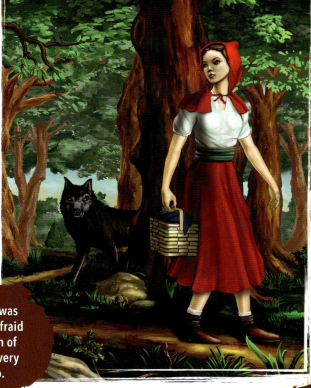

When "Little Red Riding Hood" was first written, people were more afraid of wolves (and werewolves) than of evil humans. Werewolves were very popular several centuries ago.

GOING TO THE DOGS

SHAPESHIFTERS

As mythical creatures go, the werewolf is a shapeshifter. That means it can change or **metamorphose**. The *bakemono* of Japan, Celtic selkies, the Navajo skin-walkers, and the Philippine *aswang* are all examples of animals able to transform into people or people who can transform into animals.

Shape-shifting not only stretches around the world, but also far back into history. Cave paintings dating back 25,000 years depict half-human, half-animal figures. Among the earliest cultures, **shamans** were believed to shift their human shape into some kind of animal, such as an owl, a raven, or a wolf. As animals, shamans were thought to experience a closer connection to spiritual worlds or divine energies. They gained the animal's strength and intelligence.

Anubis, the ancient Egyptian god of the afterlife, has a man's body and the head of a jackal.

HUNT OR BE HUNTED

As far back as 45,000 years ago, during the Paleolithic or Stone Age, nomadic peoples worshipped the superior powers of predatory animals. These beasts were bigger, stronger, faster, and equipped with fangs and claws. Archaeological evidence suggests that warriors clothed themselves in animal skins and made helmets from the hollowed skulls of predators. Such practices supposedly endowed these people with a predator's many strengths.

In a world divided into those who hunt and those who are hunted, predators needed to embody superior traits.

Viking warriors also channeled animal spirits by wearing their hides. The *berserker* wore bear skins, while the *úlfhednar* wore wolf coats.

FAST FACT

According to Norse mythology, the wisest of gods, Odin, created the first wolves, Geri and Freki, to accompany him on hunting expeditions. Later, when Odin created the first man and woman, he instructed them to learn from the wolves on how to survive.

EERILY ALIKE

Ancient tribes also honored the wolf by naming themselves after it. Luvians, Lucanians, Dacians, and Hyrcanians thought of themselves as "wolf men" or "people of wolves." That is, they believed they descended from wolves.

The desire to be part wolf is hardly surprising. Wolves are also startlingly similar to people. They are intelligent, wily, and communicative. Like people, they partner up to handle parenting while so many other species leave offspring to one parent. Wolves use teamwork to problem solve and hunt animals many times their size. From this evolutionary standpoint, the human fascination with wolfish transformations makes a lot of sense.

PUPPY LOVE

Valentine's Day may have ties to an ancient wolf festival known in the Roman Empire as Lupercalia. Every February 15, men dressed in wolf costumes and chased women through the streets, whipping them with leather straps.

Today, Saint Valentine's Day is celebrated with gifts of flowers, chocolate, and greeting cards. A red heart is the symbol for this day.

MAN'S BEST FRIEND?

Researchers have been able to trace humans' partnership with the canine family back at least 130,000 years. Wolves that did not eat people eventually learned they could eat our scraps and leftovers if they protected us from other predators.

Rich scholarly debate abounds as to whether humans domesticated the wolf or wild dog, or whether the wolf chose to domesticate itself.

FAST FACT
Geneticists speculate from skeletal remains that ancient dogs were quite large — probably the size of an Irish wolfhound. On all fours, a wolfhound can stand nearly 3 feet (1 m) tall, but on its hind legs, it looms over 7 feet (2 m)!

The partnership between wolves and humans has proven to be variable. Were wolves opportunists?

THE FARMER IN THE DELL

Despite not knowing who started the friendship, scientists are certain the bond was cemented around 12,000 years ago. Archaeologists have found family burials that included a domestic dog from about that time.

Soon after, the nomadic lifestyle of hunting and gathering gave way to **agrarian** societies, a way of life based on agriculture. This lifestyle involved living in one fixed place in order to cultivate crops. Farming also went hand in hand with domesticating other animals such as pigs, cows, goats, and chickens. Interestingly, as civilization settled down, society's relationship with the wolf and shape-shifting also changed.

> Humans possess about 6 million olfactory (smelling) receptors that send scent signals to our brains. But a dog's nose has up to 300 million olfactory receptors!

FALL FROM GRACE

While prehistoric peoples revered the wolf for its cunning hunting prowess, civilized farming peoples despised the animal for almost exactly the same reason. Wolves stalked flocks of sheep and herds of cows. They plucked chickens out of pens and goats from stalls. In so doing, wolves steadily transformed from superior, heroic deities to deadly, conniving enemies. Rather than worship wolves, humans began to hunt them mercilessly.

Wolves began to follow humans for sources of food.

FAST FACT

Canis lupis, the gray timber wolf, is the most common and recognizable of all wolf species. It is ferociously huge, with a body measuring 7 feet (2 m), plus another 2 feet (61 cm) of tail! It can weigh up to 150 pounds (68 kg) and kills bison and elk with ease.

GLOBAL WOLF HUNT

When Christianity became the dominant world religion, wolves were classified as pure evil and in need of extermination. What resulted was a global wolf hunt. Mass killings of wolves were carried out with much success over many centuries. These attitudes and practices traveled to North America with the first settlers. The fledgling United States government turned wolf hunting into a lucrative trade in the late 1800s. When profitable cattle ranching became the national obsession in the West, the government demanded the wolf's extermination.

In 1975, the International Union for the Conservation of Nature and Natural Resources confirmed the mass extirpation of the wolf in much of Europe. Other studies found the wolf had all but vanished in the United States. And yet, wiping out one enemy did little to diminish the myth of the werewolf. In fact, the myth got scarier.

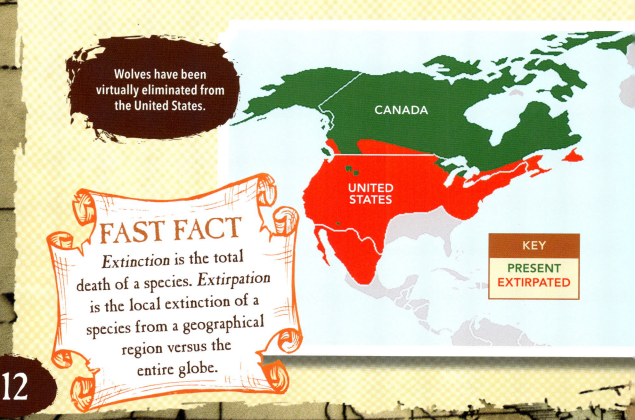

Wolves have been virtually eliminated from the United States.

FAST FACT

Extinction is the total death of a species. *Extirpation* is the local extinction of a species from a geographical region versus the entire globe.

BELIEFS UNLEASHED

CRIME AND PUNISHMENT

Even as wolves began to disappear from forests around the world, they reemerged in stories, playing the part of pure evil. To be transformed into a wolf was now a punishment, not an honor.

THE WRATH OF ISHTAR

The Mesopotamian *Epic of Gilgamesh* is considered one of the world's oldest surviving myths recorded in writing. (Much of Mesopotamia existed in what is now Iraq.) According to the tale, the goddess Ishtar punished a shepherd, transforming him into a wolf. Essentially, she made him the destroyer of his own livelihood.

In Mesopotamian mythology, Ishtar was an angel-like goddess of love, power, and war.

13

KING LYCAON

Seven hundred years after *Gilgamesh*, the oldest tales surviving from ancient Greece maintain the belief that shape-shifting from man to wolf remains a steep penalty imposed by the gods. The myth of King Lycaon is perhaps the best known. Lycaon meets with a beggar who claims to be the god Zeus in disguise. Unconvinced, Lycaon tests the beggar by serving him a special supper of roasted human flesh.

Zeus is neither fooled nor amused. He kills all of Lycaon's sons with bolts of lightning and turns the king into a yowling, bloodthirsty wolf-man. Lycaon's arms become legs. His hair becomes fur. Physically, he is every part the wolf minus a tail. Only his hard face and bright, ferocious eyes retain their human appearance.

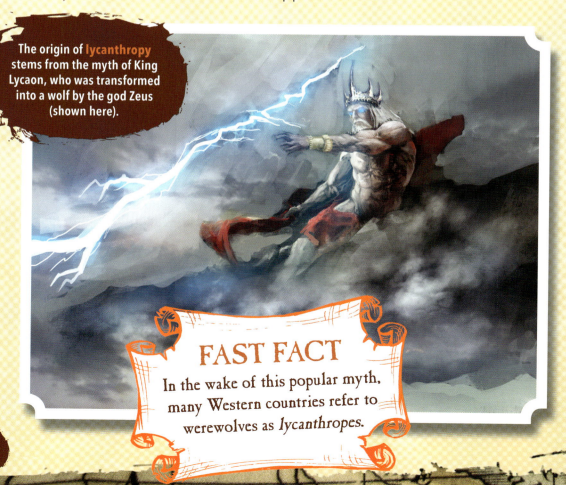

The origin of **lycanthropy** stems from the myth of King Lycaon, who was transformed into a wolf by the god Zeus (shown here).

FAST FACT
In the wake of this popular myth, many Western countries refer to werewolves as *lycanthropes*.

WHEN VIKINGS GO HIKING

The Norse mythology once prevalent across Scandinavian countries such as Iceland, Denmark, Norway, and Sweden has been largely preserved in the form of sagas, or epic poems. These poems were recited long before they were ever written down.

The *Volsunga Saga* stands out as one full of shape-shifting tales. One part of the saga depicts how Sigmund and his son, Sintjotli, found magical wolf pelts in the woods. When they tied these skins around their waists, father and son transformed into wolves. They enjoyed all the strength, cunning, and valor of the creature. At the end of their transformation, the men readily burned the pelts to ashes.

Scandinavian sagas tell of *kveldulf*, the "evening-wolf," which may derive from a historical figure, Kveldulf Bjalfason. Kveldulf was a *berserker* of the ninth century. Some sources claim these warriors actually transformed into bloodthirsty beasts during battles.

Berserkers were fierce warriors who dressed in animal skins to assume greater power and killer instincts. Today, we know that they also drank hallucinogenic potions, which made them truly go berserk!

15

EL LOBIZON

In South America, tales of *el lobizon* are popular in Argentina, Brazil, Paraguay, and Uruguay. This shapeshifter myth goes back to the native Guarani people of Paraguay who tell of seven monsters, the seventh standing out as a hideously deformed god of death. As European people conquered South American lands and settled there, the tale of *el lobizon* merged with their werewolf myths. The result was a belief that the seventh son in any family was sure to become a *lobizon*—especially if he was born on the night of a full moon.

HULI JING

It might be easy to assume that all were-beasts are male, but the opposite is sometimes true. In Chinese mythology, *huli jing* are fox spirits that typically transform into beautiful women. There are many different versions of these were-women, who can be good or evil. In some cases, they are guardians of the underworld. Luckily, they are easy to recognize, because like most were-beasts, they are missing a tail.

Bitten is a novel by Canadian writer Kelley Armstrong that follows Elena Michaels, the world's only female werewolf. The book became a TV series spanning three seasons, starring Laura Vandervoort (second from the right) as Michaels.

The *loup garou* is the French version of the werewolf. *Loup* is the French word for wolf, and *garou* is an Old French word for werewolf.

FAST FACT

In Hindu folklore, stormy winds can metamorphose into werewolves. Known as *rakshasas*, these howling mythical creatures are covered in bristling, coarse hair. Their protruding teeth are built to tear and devour human flesh!

BAD LUCK

The Norse sagas and South American legends demonstrate an important element in werewolf myths: the person who transforms is not always a willing participant. Magic or curses befall unlucky and unsuspecting victims, forever ruining their lives. For example, the *loup garou* of France feels guilty when it slaughters innocent life. It wishes it could end its werewolf curse. But in other versions of the werewolf myth, the shapeshifter may be all too willing to change into a murderous monster.

WITCHES AND WIZARDS

The *bultungin* of central Sudan in Africa is a were-hyena. The word actually translates as, "I change myself into a hyena," which implies the use of magic to transform oneself willingly. Across many regions of the continent, people believed witches and wizards regularly transformed into *bultungin*. Old legends hinted at entire villages populated entirely with were-hyenas. Elsewhere in Africa, hyenas were believed to transform themselves into humans.

VAMPIRES VERSUS WEREWOLVES

We associate vampire lore with the Eastern European countries. Yet the literature suggests that werewolves emerged first. *Vukodlak, vlkodlak, vlkoslak, vrykolaka*—all are words from the Slavic, Czech, Serbian, and Greek languages used to label vampires. They actually mean "wolf's fur" or "wolf's hair." Wolves often dug corpses out of shallow graves. Passersby or mourners who stumbled upon a wolf in a grave where a corpse should have been thought that some kind of demonic transformation had taken place. Over time, the "risen dead" morphed into people's imaginations as vampires, and the wolves lurking around graveyards became vampires' sworn enemies.

In a contest between a werewolf and a vampire, who do you think would win?

DANGEROUS DESIRES

In Mexico, were-beasts are commonly referred to as *nahual* or *nagual* (pronounced na-HWAL). The *nahual* myth varies widely. It can be a guardian spirit that takes on the form of a deer, eagle, bobcat, or some other powerful animal. Alternatively, the *nahual* is a man who transforms into a beast and deliberately harms others. Similarly, in Native American folklore, the *wendigo* is entirely malevolent. Sometimes it is a spirit that possesses the souls of people and turns them into **cannibals**. Sometimes it is a shape-shifting man-beast continually thirsting for blood.

IN FACT AND FICTION

Stephanie Meyer's *Twilight Saga* was a global phenomenon featuring vampires and werewolves. Meyers adapted Native American myths from the Pacific Northwest to create werewolf packs with impressive powers and instincts. For instance, shape-shifting legends from the Quileute people, who lived in what is now the state of Washington, are echoed in the *Twilight* wolves' ability to heal quickly and communicate telepathically.

Taylor Lautner became one of today's most famous werewolves when he portrayed Jacob Black in the *Twilight* movies.

THE WORLD'S WER-ZOO

Across Earth's vast terrains, wherever wolves were not common, other were-beasts arose to take their place in legends. In Mexico, tigers, eagles, and serpents were believed to morph with men and women. Vulture, tiger, and jaguar were-monsters were feared in Central and South America. In India and China, were-tigers were popular, while in Africa, were-hyenas and were-leopards reigned supreme. Crocodiles, coyotes, buffalo, and other formidable beasts made excellent were-monsters elsewhere in the world.

> If a creature was common to an area and feared for being deadly, it was likely to wind up on the were-beast roster.

LA CALCHONA

Usually, only the fiercest and scariest animals are inducted into the hallowed halls of were-beast lore. *La calchona* of Chile is the exception to the rule. She is part-woman, part-sheep. The story goes that a woman, by dabbling in a bit of witchcraft, once created a magic cream in order to become a night-rambling sheep. Her husband, who refused to have the wool pulled over his eyes, dumped out the magic cream and left her. The woman retrieved only enough cream to return her face to its human shape; thus she forever roams as *la calchona*.

MARKING TERRITORY

UP TO NO GOOD

Across the mythical werewolf landscape, there are certain signposts familiar to just about every culture. First, becoming a werewolf requires special circumstances. Second, the moon often plays a role in creating werewolves. Finally, if a werewolf cannot be cured, then it has to be killed.

EVIL ASSOCIATIONS

Many shamans, witches, wizards, and sorcerers may have been healers, but with the spread of Christianity, witchcraft was seen as a challenge and a contradiction to religious doctrines. It was condemned as the work of the devil. Likewise, the wolf was seen as an agent of the devil, sent to plague humankind with destruction and evil. What is more, witches had the power to turn people into werewolves and send them on evil errands.

Vargamor were old women, possibly witches, who lived in the forests of Sweden and used spells to transform and control werewolves.

RECIPE FOR TROUBLE

Once upon a time in Russia, Finland, Sweden, and Armenia, there were allegedly wizards, sorcerers, and warlocks who magically transformed into werewolves and carried out horrible murders. Surviving records found in Siberia detail the ingredients needed to make a werewolf potion. First, set an iron pot over a fire and combine several ounces of hemlock, henbane, saffron, poppy seeds, aloe, opium, asafetida, solanum, and parsley.

While this might sound like a salad from a health food store, it is actually a poisonous concoction. Many of the ingredients are dangerous biochemicals that can cut off signals between the brain and body. They induce numbness or tingling, as well as powerful hallucinations. Similar recipes exist across Europe for potions and salves which, if consumed or spread over the skin, guarantee transformation.

THIRSTY?

In 1562, Italian physicist Giambattista della Porta noted that drinking wine laced with various toxic plants and herbs such as aconite (wolfsbane) and belladonna (deadly nightshade) would produce powerful shape-shifting hallucinations.

aconite

belladonna

OPEN WIDE

In parts of Transylvania, Hungary, Austria, and Czechoslovakia, old legends warn against eating certain flowers that might trigger a lycanthropic episode. Lilies of the valley, marigolds, and azaleas were on the list.

Perhaps more powerful than plants was any kind of contact with a wolf. A wolf bite was thought to turn a person into a werewolf. Eating the raw flesh of a wolf, especially a rabid one, was sure to result in lycanthropy. Drinking water from a wolf's pond or pool was another cause. And, as demonstrated in the Norse tale of Sigmund and Sintjotli, wearing a wolf pelt, or girdle, could turn someone into a werewolf.

If you got bitten by a wolf, chances are you would turn into a werewolf.

A FULL MOON

The moon has enjoyed a close, magical connection to many shapeshifters, including werewolves. Many myths claim the cycles of the moon trigger a werewolf's metamorphosis.

Being born on the night of a full moon was considered a surefire way to make a werewolf.

With its ever-changing crescents and spheres, the moon, or *luna* in several other languages, is a kind of shapeshifter. And long before science could explain how, ancient observers did not miss the moon's observable pull on ocean tides. The moon, it must have seemed, was a magical object.

Indeed, the ancient Greeks believed the moon pulled not just on the oceans, but also on the liquids inside the human brain. Too much pulling and sloshing might scramble the mind and affect clear thinking. A person affected by the moon went mad and was called a "lunatic."

FAST FACT
In Romania, the *vârcolac* is a mythical werewolf that causes eclipses when it swallows the sun and moon.

SILVER BULLETS

If you were tasked with killing a werewolf, you might follow the conventions of most Hollywood horror films and try shooting it with a silver bullet. Before firearms existed, silver weapons were the go-to choice for proper and effective werewolf destruction. Silver was thought to harbor lunar powers, probably because it reflects a silky, milky sheen similar to moonlight.

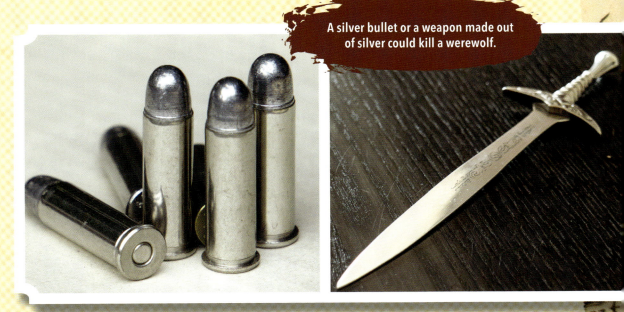

A silver bullet or a weapon made out of silver could kill a werewolf.

If silver was not on hand, then just about any sharp or blunt weapon could be employed to stab or bludgeon a werewolf to death. And to ensure it did not become a vampire, many Eastern European legends suggested decapitating the beast and burning its body to ashes.

Curiously, the world's mythologies have less to say about killing a werewolf and much more about how to cure it.

A BITTER PILL TO SWALLOW

According to *De Virtutibus Herbarum*, a seventeenth-century medical textbook, the best way to cure the curse of lycanthropy was to wrap a wolf's tooth in a bay leaf and wear it as an amulet. This **remedy** offered the bonus of supposedly warding off bullies.

The *Medicina de Quadrupedibus*, another seventeenth-century medical work, applies a contradictory logic: that which curses also cures. The text suggests wearing a wolf girdle to cure one's lycanthropic tendencies. If that didn't work, then perhaps sleeping with a wolf's head under one's pillow might do the trick. Other medical books swore by eating burnt and powdered wolf skull to end the werewolf curse.

Eating powdered wolf's skull had the added benefit of relieving arthritis.

dried mugwort

MIXED PRESCRIPTIONS

Elsewhere in the world, cures were all over the map! Among the Dutch, it was thought that scolding the werewolf or calling the monster by its human name might cure it. Other legends instructed people to strategically spill just three drops of its blood. Still others insisted on locking the werewolf away for nine years to prevent it from attacking anyone.

In ancient India, healers adopted a more culinary approach. If a werewolf bit or scratched a victim, the wound was to be **cauterized**. This was often accomplished with scalding hot butter, which the victim also had to drink. In China, priests burned mugwort, a species of the wormwood plant. Then they put the ashes on the bite mark. If that did not work, then they would rub dog brains on the wound.

ALIVE AND KICKING

Across Europe, cures focused on removing the wolf-demon from a person's body. This might be achieved through bloodletting or drinking lots of vinegar to induce vomiting. However, throughout the Middle Ages, the most advanced studies in medical science came from Arab physicians, who prescribed pressing a scalding hot branding iron against the forehead of anyone suspected of being a werewolf. Is it any wonder so many of those suffering with werewolf symptoms died during treatment?

But why is the werewolf treated rather than exterminated? To find out, we must explore the biology and **pathology** behind the myth.

WHEN IN ROME

In ancient Rome, werewolf bites were treated with salt, pickle, burned hair from a dog's tail, or maggots plucked from a dog's carcass. When those methods failed, the werewolf had to eat a dog's head, or rooster brains, or goose fat, or chicken poop. As a last resort, doctors made a hellebore (type of flower) poultice and put it on the victim's rear end.

Many cultures around the world consider maggots a tasty treat!

DIGGING UP THE TRUTH

SETTLING DOWN

The human transition from the nomadic to the agrarian lifestyle delivered more than abundant food harvests. Eating more meant people could have larger families. These families settled into collective communities. Villages grew into towns and cities and suddenly, infectious diseases spread with greater ease.

Not only that, early agriculture meant humans lived in closer, daily contact with animals. As a result, the **microbes** living inside animals mutated and took up residence in the human population.

Animals such as cows and sheep can spread disease to humans, such as the so-called mad cow disease. Once transmitted to humans, it is called Creutzfeldt-Jakob disease (CJD). CJD destroys the brain and has no cure.

Animals such as sheep, goats, cows, pigs, and chickens were raised close to humans.

SICK IDEAS

Some diseases that come from animals are caused by **viruses**. These include Ebola, SARS, HIV, and swine flu.

Without the aid of scientific reasoning and tools such as microscopes, ancient peoples had no way to understand the sudden rise of sickness. No way except through myths, that is. About the time humankind declared the once-revered wolf its enemy, mass outbreaks of animal-transmitted diseases cycled through cities. The obvious explanation was that wolves were evil, and they had the power to possess the human body. And so a myth was born.

RABIES

The mythical conclusion might appear ridiculous until you consider rabies. Rabies is a disease that seems to have emerged first in bats before spreading to wolves and dogs. As viruses go, rabies is probably one of the world's creepiest. You don't catch it from just a little sneeze or cough. You get it when you are bitten by an infected animal (or person).

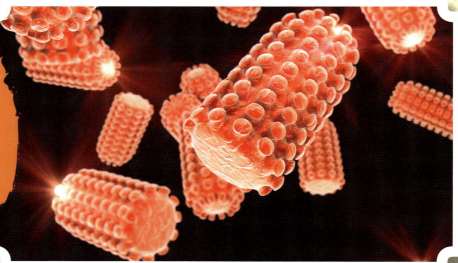

This image of the rabies virus reveals its eerie resemblance to a silver bullet: a cylindrical shell designed to travel through the nervous system.

Symptoms of rabies include frothing at the mouth, moaning, growling, and howling.

FAST FACT
In 2011, the National Archives in England released documents regarding Operation Werewolf, a World War II Nazi scheme to commit mass murder by injecting poison into coffee, chocolate, and aspirin.

ONCE BITTEN

Unlike nearly all other viruses known to science, rabies does not travel through the blood. Instead, it crawls along an electric transmission network that relays signals between the brain and the body of a creature. Traveling only up to 1 inch (2 cm) a day, the rabies virus creeps from the bite wound to the brain. When it arrives, it sort of "howls" back to the old site of the bite mark. Even if the wound has healed, the bite marks will burn, tingle, ache, or go numb. Many victims report feeling as though they were bitten twice in the same spot.

Inside the brain, the virus bends and warps the mind. Victims become hyper-aggressive because the virus fills their thoughts with the need to attack. In other words, rabies creates werewolf characteristics in its victims.

To ancient peoples, a rabies infection would have looked like the curse of beastly behavior passing from the animal to the victim. The myth explained the inexplicable.

BLACK DEATH

Perhaps the greatest disease catastrophe in human history is still the outbreak of bubonic plague — the Black Death — in the fourteenth century. From 1347 to 1350, the Black Death ravaged three entire continents, killing more than 200 million people.

The plague repeatedly disappeared and reappeared over the next several centuries. Each time it struck, werewolf and witchcraft hysterias also erupted. Tens of thousands of men and women (some 30,000 in France alone) were accused of being either witches or werewolves, or both. They stood trial, and once convicted, the allegedly guilty werewolves were beaten, hanged, and burned.

FAST FACT

In the past, most scientists believed that the bubonic plague was spread by rats. Actually, it was the fleas on the rats that were the culprits.

The doctors who treated victims of the bubonic plague sometimes wore pointed masks, which they filled with sweet-smelling items so that the foul stench of the victims would not smell as bad.

The most famous hellhound is Cerberus from Greek mythology, the three-headed beast that guarded the gates of Hades.

BLACK DOGS

The Black Death also helped revive the myth of the Hellhound. The plague was deadly. Bodies piled up like firewood in the streets of towns and cities. Stray dogs and wolves scavenged off these corpses. The result: the myth of the Black Dog. If seen, this demon dog was considered an omen of bad luck and misfortune, even death. Often called the Hellhound, these creatures were thought to be supernatural with glowing red eyes, a fur coat as black as coal, and razor-sharp teeth. They were capable of great strength and speed and they were huge—as large as a calf or even a horse!

By 1665, the city of London passed the "six-feet-under law," requiring that all bodies be buried no less than 6 feet (2 m) underground in order to deter cadaver scavengers.

SHIFT IN THE MYTH

Jean Grenier was only 13 when he was convicted of being a werewolf. He was condemned to serve life in prison. Grenier's tragic case marks an important shift in Europe's thoughts on werewolves.

The seventeenth-century French court that tried Grenier seemed to think the boy's delusions were less demonic and more likely a mental abnormality. The brain, it seemed, could malfunction without magical interference. Reviews of Grenier's symptoms have led some contemporary psychiatrists to suggest that the boy may have struggled with a severe form of autism, a vastly complex neural condition of the brain.

FAST FACT

In 1978, in southern Brazil, 16-year-old Eliana Barbosa was nailed to a cross for three days while priests tried to exorcise the "wolf demon" she claimed had taken over her soul.

Fedor Jeftichew, or Jo-Jo the Dog-Faced Man, was 16 when he journeyed from Russia to perform in P.T. Barnum's world-famous circus.

HAIR-RAISING FACTS

If you've ever heard of circus "freaks" like the Bearded Lady or the Dog-Faced Boy, then you may have heard of people with Congenital Generalized Hypertrichosis Terminalis (CGHT). CGHT is also known as werewolf syndrome. This disease causes extremely thick hair growth to sprout all over the body. The condition can also spur the ears to elongate and the mouth and lips to swell. The result is a werewolf resemblance.

Although rare, the disease has been around for a very long time and probably led to some eyewitness accounts of werewolf sightings.

EDIBLE INSANITY

The last suspect on the list of werewolf causes is ergot, a fungus that, if ingested, stirs up violent hallucinations. Many people report sensations of their body transforming into some kind of predator, such as a wolf or tiger. In medieval Europe, ergot frequently contaminated the rye and wheat grains people ate. It caused epidemics of a condition known as Saint Anthony's Fire, the symptoms of which included painful blisters and gangrene in the fingers and toes. As recently as the 1950s, France experienced an outbreak of ergotism. Even then, sufferers reported hallucinations.

When inexplicable events happen, people naturally look for causes. They piece together observations that appear to be connected. From this process, a myth emerges. The werewolf myth served as a likely explanation for conditions that were caused by invisible germs. Werewolves would also become a **scapegoat** for humankind's diseases.

FAST FACT

Aconite, or wolfsbane, is a toxic plant. As a biochemical, it causes rabies-like symptoms: foamy saliva and wild disorientation.

LEADER
OF THE PACK

KIBBLES AND BITS

The winter of 1521 was bleak, icy, and bloody in Besançon, France. Pierre Bourgot and Michel Verdung confessed to their crimes before a packed audience in an oak-timbered courtroom. They admitted being werewolves who derived their powers from the devil. And they admitted that while transformed, they murdered and mutilated many victims. "Michel thought the girl's flesh particularly delicious although it gave him indigestion," Bourgot recounted as he recalled their slaughter of a four-year-old child. The two men were executed, as were many others.

STRAY DOG

In 1536, Gilles Garnier went on a four-month rampage in the village of Dole. He killed and consumed the flesh of children. According to 50 witnesses, he howled at the moon after each killing. Garnier was finally captured and burned alive in 1537.

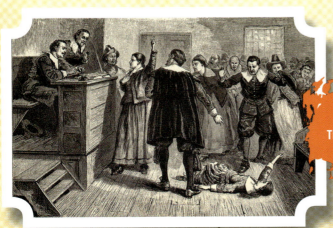

Many witches were considered werewolves or able to control werewolves. Thousands were tortured, convicted in courts, and executed during the Middle Ages.

RESIDENT EVIL

Peter Stump (also spelled Stub, Stube, Stubbe, or Stumpf) attacked, mauled, and murdered many people over two-and-a-half decades in Germany. According to Stump's testimony, he was a werewolf. One pamphlet that circulated the country like a modern tabloid newspaper claimed that Stump murdered 13 women in five years. Stump also confessed to cannibalism. Stump was executed on October 31, 1589. The authorities tied him to a wheel and pulled off his skin with hot pincers. They shattered his bones and cut off his head. Finally, they burned what was left of his body.

During the sixteenth and seventeenth centuries, the wheel was used to torture and execute people, as shown in this 1633 illustration.

JUDGE, JURY, AND EXECUTIONER

These three prominent werewolf trials show how people tend to blame their sins and crimes on others. The werewolf was blamed for the greedy and violent acts of convicted criminals. Throughout all the witch and werewolf trials, the judges acted with the same beastly violence as the accused.

MONSTROUS MEDICINE

This notion of the shadowy beast lurking inside everyone has proven vital to the ongoing survival of the werewolf myth. Unlike other mythical monsters, the werewolf never found a comfortable home in printed storybooks. He remained caged up in medical books and court documents. But in the 1800s, the beast broke free and ran **rampant** through popular imagination.

EVIL INSIGHT

The 1800s were years of unprecedented change on a global scale. New technologies flooded into people's lives, upending all the old ways of thinking. The previous century had ushered in the Enlightenment, or the Age of Reason, when scientific methods involving experiments, hypotheses, tests, measurements, and massive information-sharing opened up new fields of research in medicine, physics, psychology, astronomy, geology, and more. The world no longer seemed mysterious and inexplicable.

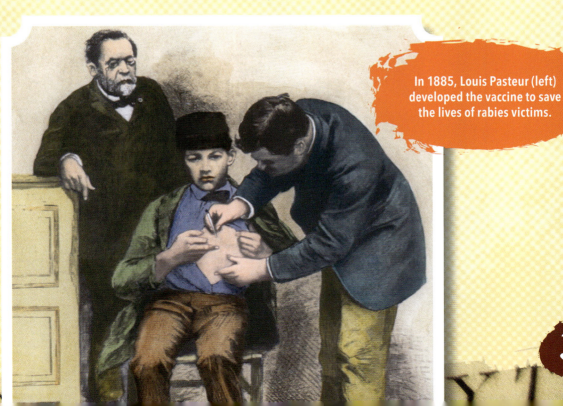

In 1885, Louis Pasteur (left) developed the vaccine to save the lives of rabies victims.

CHARLES DARWIN

In 1859, following decades of arduous research, Charles Darwin published *On the Origin of Species*. In the text, Darwin laid out his radical and controversial theory of evolution, the process by which organisms constantly mutate over time, creating new kinds organisms—the scientific version of shape-shifting. Recent discoveries in other scientific fields supported Darwin's theory.

With Darwin's theory of evolution catching on, archaeologists swiftly realized the half-human, half-ape bones they were unearthing weren't the remnants of people disfigured by some strange disease. They were, in fact, humankind's early ancestors.

FAST FACT
Charles Darwin began studying to become a doctor. But he couldn't stand the sight of blood!

Charles Darwin (1809–1882) was an English naturalist, geologist, and biologist.

A MONSTROUS REALIZATION

How could civilized, elegant, intelligent humans have descended from apes? The public criticized Darwin and his supporters. But over time, the evidence outweighed the doubts. Humans, like werewolves, were partial animals without tails. And like werewolves, humans were capable of great atrocities, as evidenced by a rash of serial killers. Jack the Ripper in London, H.H. Holmes in Chicago, and Joseph Vacher in France are just three examples.

DOUBLE AGENTS

In 1886, *The Strange Case of Dr. Jekyll and Mr. Hyde*, a novella by Robert Louis Stevenson, gave the werewolf myth new life. The scientist Dr. Jekyll wants to eliminate his dark, inner beast using scientific medical means. Like wizards and sorcerers of old, he makes a potion that is supposed to eliminate the primitive part of him that descended from apes. Instead, the potion backfires. Jekyll transforms into a half-man, half-beast monster yearning for evil. Stevenson's descriptions of the monster, named Mr. Hyde, mingle traits that are both wolfish and ape-like.

The public was appropriately horrified. The werewolf finally earned its place in print beyond the medical field.

This theatrical poster shows Dr. Jekyll transforming into Mr. Hyde (right).

Although there have been many "sightings," there has yet to be definitive proof that Bigfoot actually exists. Yet the myth continues.

THE YETI, SASQUATCH, AND BIGFOOT

First, the werewolf clawed its way into what is known as pulp fiction—short, cheap, sensational publications once called "penny dreadfuls" or "penny bloods." The names indicate not only their price, but also their content. In pulp fiction, the werewolf carried on the Jekyll-and-Hyde tradition, spawning a whole new generation of **cryptids**—monsters such as the Yeti, Sasquatch, and Bigfoot. These creatures mixed human, ape, and wolf traits.

In the early 1900s, a boom of werewolf tales terrified audiences. The most popular was penned by English writer Algernon Blackwood. But if we think of the werewolf as an evolving symbol of humankind's bigger problems or worst habits, then it makes sense that a creature representing humanity's evil, murderous, dark side would surge to even greater popularity around the same time the world descended into two of its most brutal wars: World Wars I and II.

HOUNDED BY FANS

In 1933, during the brief period between the two great wars, American author Guy Endore lived through the poverty of the Great Depression long enough to write *The Werewolf of Paris*. Once published, the novel soared to the top of the bestseller list.

The phenomenal novel inspired countless more werewolf tales in comic books, which functioned as modernized penny dreadfuls. They were also inexpensive and full of sensational stories. This time, the stories were told through jaw-dropping artwork, which inspired the moviemakers of Hollywood.

The 2004 film *Van Helsing* paid tribute to the werewolf and monster mania of the 1930s and 1940s by combining them all into one epic story. The movie grossed $300 million worldwide—strong evidence that old myths are eternally popular.

Hugh Jackman starred in the 2004 *Van Helsing* movie.

FAST FACT

Rick Baker, a Hollywood makeup artist, deserves ample credit for making the werewolf a horror movie icon. His artistry created three of the most terrifying werewolf transformation scenes—in *The Howling*, *An American Werewolf in London*, and Michael Jackson's "Thriller" music video.

BEST IN SHOW

A slew of big-hit monster movies spanning almost five decades kicked off with the 1941 classic, *The Wolf Man,* starring Lon Chaney. The 1980s witnessed a fresh resurgence of werewolf blockbusters including *The Howling* (1981), *An American Werewolf in London* (1981), and *Teen Wolf* (1985). Many of these films were so popular that they were remade in the 1990s and 2000s. As if coming around full circle, the werewolf figures emerging in more recent movies and books seem to be restoring the myth to its original, prehistoric place of honor and reverence.

Time passes. Civilizations rise and fall. Diseases come and go. But the werewolf has always remained. Over and over, the werewolf emerges as our mythical tutor and scapegoat. We cyclically slaughter the monster and revive it from near extinction—just like the wolf. Perhaps this is how we avoid facing our inner demons and dark desires. Then again, this may be the only way to slowly extinguish our evils.

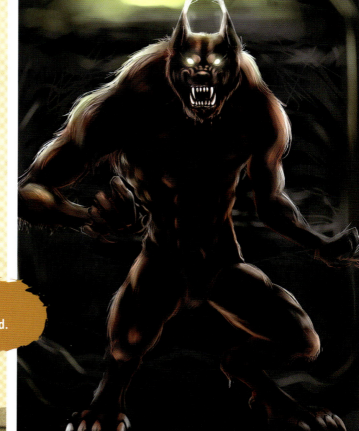

The werewolf exists to transform us and our world.

WEREWOLF MYTHS ACROSS THE MAP

Here are some of the places where werewolf myths originated.

MAP KEY

1. Argentina
2. Armenia
3. Austria
4. Brazil
5. Chile
6. China
7. Czechoslovakia
8. Denmark
9. Egypt
10. England
11. Finland
12. France
13. Germany
14. Greece
15. Hollywood
16. Hungary
17. Iceland
18. Iraq
19. India
20. Italy
21. Japan
22. Mexico
23. Netherlands
24. Norway
25. Paraguay
26. Philippines
27. Romania; Transylvania
28. Russia
29. Saudi Arabia
30. Serbia
31. Siberia
32. Sudan
33. Sweden
34. United States
35. Uruguay
36. Washington (state)

45

GLOSSARY

agrarian relating to farmers or farming; agricultural

cannibal any animal, including humans, that feeds on the flesh of its own species

cauterize to burn with a hot iron or a chemical substance, usually to destroy infected tissue

cryptids folkloric creatures studied by cryptozoologists, who search for the existence of fairy-tale figures

lycanthropy the assumption of the form and characteristics of a wolf through witchcraft or magic

metamorphose to change completely in form and appearance

microbes microorganisms, including bacteria, fungi, and viruses, that cause disease

pathology the study of diseases, their causes and effects

rampant not checked in growth or spread

remedy a medicine or treatment

scapegoat a person or thing that is blamed for something

shaman a priest or priestess who uses magic to cure the sick, control natural events, or foretell the future

virus a tiny infectious agent that is too small to be seen except through an electron microscope

FURTHER INFORMATION

BOOKS

Heiligman, Deborah. *Charles and Emma: The Darwins' Leap of Faith*. Portland, Ore.: Square Fish Publishing, 2011.

Howison, Del. *When Werewolves Attack: A Field Guide to Dispatching Ravenous Flesh-Ripping Beasts*. New York: JABberwocky Literary Agency, Inc., 2013.

Leitich Smith, Cynthia. *Feral Nights*. Somerville, Mass.: Candlewick, 2014.

Stevenson, Robert Louis. *Dr. Jekyll and Mr. Hyde*. New York: Start Publishing LLC, 2017.

Valentino, Serena. *How to Be a Werewolf: The Claws-on Guide for the Modern Lycanthrope*. Somerville, Mass.: Candlewick, 2011.

WEBSITES

Learn all about real-life wolves here!
http://kids.nationalgeographic.com/animals/gray-wolf/#gray

Visit the International Wolf Center here!
http://www.wolf.org/wolf-info/wild-kids/fun-facts/

Explore fairy tales and myths from around the world at this awesome site!
http://www.worldoftales.com/

Publisher's note to educators and parents: Our editors have carefully reviewed these websites to ensure that they are suitable for students. Many websites change frequently, however, and we cannot guarantee that a site's future contents will continue to meet our high standards of quality and educational value. Be advised that students should be closely supervised whenever they access the Internet.

INDEX

An American Werewolf in London (film), 43, 44
Armstrong, Kelley, 16
Baker, Rick, 43
Barbosa, Elena, 34
Barnum, P.T., 35
Bitten (novel & TV series), 16
Black Death, 32, 33
Blackwood, Algernon, 42
Bourgot, Pierre, 37
cannibalism, 19, 38
Chaney, Lon, 44
Creutzfeldt-Jakob Disease (CJD), 29
curses, 17, 26, 31
Darwin, Charles, 40, 41
della Porta, Giambattista, 20
diseases, 29, 30, 32, 35, 40, 44
Endore, Guy, 43
Garnier, Gilles, 37
Gilgamesh, Epic of (poem), 13, 14
Grenier, Jean, 34
Hellhound, 33
Holmes, H.H., 41
Howling, The (film), 43, 44
Jack the Ripper, 41
Jackman, Hugh, 43
Jackson, Michael, 43
Jeftichew, Fedor, 35
Lautner, Taylor, 19
"Little Red Riding Hood" (story), 5
lycanthropy, 14, 23, 26
magic, 15, 17, 18, 20, 22, 24, 34
Meyer, Stephanie, 19
moon effect, 4, 16, 21, 24, 25, 27
On the Origin of Species (book), 40
Pasteur, Louis, 39
shapeshifters, 6, 10, 14, 15, 16, 17, 19, 22, 24
Sigmund and Sintjotli, 15, 23
silver weapons, 25, 30
Star Wars (films), 35
Stevenson, Robert Louis, 41
Strange Case of Dr. Jekyll and Mr. Hyde (novel), 41
Stump, Peter, 38
Teen Wolf (film), 44
"Three Little Pigs" (story), 43
Twilight Saga (novels & films), 19
Vacher, Joseph, 41
Van Helsing (film), 44
Vandervoort, Laura, 16
Verdung, Michel, 37
Werewolf of Paris (novel), 43
witchcraft, 18, 20, 21, 32, 37, 38
"Wolf and the Seven Goats, The" (story), 43
Wolf Man, The (film), 44